I read your book. My husband is like putty in
my hands now. Who knew all I needed to do was
mess with him a little?

Leslie Swart
Senior Partner, Blue Skye Lending
Lakewood Ranch, Florida

Chris Angermann has put together an easy-reading
but explosive book that takes a close look at a lot of
the BS (belief systems) cluttering the world today.
If you are looking for political correctness, this book
is not for you. If you are looking for unique and refreshing
concepts on life, don't miss the chance to read this book!

Rik Feeney
Author, *Writing Books for Fun, Fame & Fortune!*

This is a SMART book. Extremely thoughtful, original and
wickedly witty, too, there is something here for every one of us
who require a more insightful self-observing ego, from time
to time.… I love this book. Because it takes so little time
to read and overflows with practical humor and wisdom,
I've found my perfect "stocking-stuffer" gift, especially
for loved ones & co-workers.

Ellen Menard
Author, *The Not So Patient Advocate*

Really enjoyed *How to Mess*, etc. Gave book
to my son who has two boys 7 and 10.

Dr. Herbert Silverstein, MD
Founder, Silverstein Institute
Sarasota, Florida

Bardolf & Company

HOW TO MESS WITH OTHERS FOR THEIR OWN GOOD

Third Edition

ISBN 978-1-938842-45-0

Copyright © 2012, 2015, 2020, 2023, 2025 by Chris Angermann

All rights reserved. No part of this book may be used or reproduced in any form or by any electronic or mechanical means, including information storage and retrieval systems, without permission in writing from the publisher.

Published by Bardolf & Company
 www.bardolfandcompany.com

Cover design by Shaw Creative
 www.shawcreativegroup.com

**To my wife, Susan,
and my son, Erik,
who make it all worthwhile**

Also by Chris Angermann

DRAMATIC MEASURES
Lessons from a Life in the Theater

THE FIGHT FOR JUSTICE
Lee Kreindler and Lockerby
(co-author with Ruth Kreindler)

All typos, redundancies
and grammar errors have
have been put into this book
intentionally for your enjoyment
in finding them.

HOW TO MESS WITH OTHERS FOR THEIR OWN GOOD

Chris Angermann

Bardolf & Company
Sarasota, Florida 2025

PREFACE TO THE THIRD (+) EDITION

In Lieu of a Fourth Iteration

The challenge with comical writing is that it can get dated rather quickly. People's memories are short, and without shared knowledge of certain historical references, events and details, some of the satire and humor will fall flat. It's the nature of the beast.

Still, when I reread my little book of advice, I realized that most of my observations and suggestions are still relevant, in a number of cases more so than before. Some rust needed to be scraped off and some stale, outmoded parts required updating. This third (+) edition does that. I have eliminated examples that may no longer resonate with current readers and added more up-to-date material.

What I never imagined was that the election of an ignorant, narcissistic, self-serving, whining vulgarian as President of the United States would coarsen public discourse to the degree it has. Donald Trump has had an uncanny ability to mess with others, but only for his own good. There is little positive calculation in any of his words or actions, except what's in it for him.

In contentious times of trouble, it is crucial to resist the flagrant excesses of those in power. But we must not go overboard in our responses—admittedly hard to do when confronted with verbal atrocities and reprehensible actions that boggle the mind. This is important, though: We must not become the mirror image of intolerance and dehumanization.

The German philosopher Nietzsche's famous dictum applies here: "Beware that, when fighting monsters, you yourself do not become a monster…for when you gaze long into the abyss, the abyss gazes also into you."

We must provide an alternative. Humor and satire can help with that.

So, let us try to restore balance and civility to our society and relearn how to respect each other's essential humanness. Someone has to break the cycle of violence, bigotry, fanaticism and ugliness. Who better to get a start on that than you and me?

More than 230 years ago, the Framers of our Constitution began the document that provides the foundation of our nation, "We the People of the United States, in Order to form a more perfect Union…"

Don't want to mess with that.

Chris Angermann
Sarasota, Florida
February 2025

HOW TO MESS WITH OTHERS FOR THEIR OWN GOOD

The only thing to do with good advice is to pass it on. It is never of any use to oneself.

—Oscar Wilde

PROLOGUE
What's Wrong With Self-Help Books

So let me be clear from the get-go. This book will not lift your spirit, improve your sex life or make you rich. It won't make you a better person or help you cope with life's challenges, although you might have more fun if you choose to follow some of its advice.

That's because it's not a self-help book.

Most bookstores have shelves heaped full of personal growth and self-development tracts, but what good are they? As the psychologist James Hillman points out in his book, *We've Had a Hundred Years of Therapy and the World's Getting Worse*, "We've had a hundred years of therapy and the world's getting worse." People are just as depressed and anxious as ever, if not more so.

Why are self-help books so useless? Why do they have so little effect even on people that go through them like boxes of Kleenex during a bad cold?

First, as the inimitable George Carlin pointed out, they're a misnomer. How can it be "self-help" when you're utilizing what someone else has written? If you're really going to help yourself, don't read a book. Go out and do something.

Second, it's really hard to get perspective on yourself. "To thine own self be true" may be sound advice—although it comes from Polonius, one of Shakespeare's great stumble-bums—but only if you know what your real self is. And who but the most elevated and advanced of human beings, someone just this side of the Dalai Lama, can claim to know that with a straight face?

Third, self-help books like to divide things up into components, like mental, emotional, physical and spiritual. Having made these distinctions, their authors think they've prepared you for the world. It's like going to a fast-food restaurant and having the server hand you the milk, ice cream, strawberries and whipped cream and say, "Here you go. Now you figure out how to put them together to make a sundae!"

The proof of the pudding is in the way these ingredients interact, overlap and blend with one another. It's what makes people unique, frustrating, unpredictable and endlessly fascinating. And self-help books never tell you how to do that because their authors have no idea. They're just as clueless as you are about how to reassemble the components!

That's why most financial gurus who tell others how to make money, make their money by telling others how to do it. And why so many relationship coaches and marriage counselors have all kinds of advice for staying together and juicing up a relationship, while they're on their own second, third or even fourth marriage.

The most egregious case—isn't that a nifty word? Egregious! I first heard it when TV sports commentator Brett Hull uttered it during the intermission of an ice hockey game. I was surprised that he'd actually used a word of more than two syllables since most sportscasters dumb down their vocabulary to grade school level. They don't want to alienate their viewers by coming off as too intellectual. But I digress.

In any case, I looked it up in the dictionary and have been using it ever since. Which brings me to my first piece of advice—if you don't know what a word in this book means, look it up!

The most egregious case in my lifetime was Maribel Morgan, an anti-feminist author and public speaker in the 1970s, who wrote *Total Woman*. She had lots of advice on how to spice up a marriage, recommending that the little woman stay at home, put on a sexy negligee for hubby arriving after work, and greet him at the door with a beer or cocktail in hand. What she neglected to tell her audiences was that she made her own marriage work by being away from home more than 200 days a year, telling other women how to become domestic(ated) sex kittens.

Most self-help books are the work of quacks.

One of the more foolish notions these snake oil salespeople have inflicted on the unwary public is the idea that, when it comes to making important changes in your life, you have to start with yourself first. These days, it's often referred to as "change from the inside out," and just about every other self-help book that comes along repeats that mantra *ad nauseam*.

Common sense would tell you that it's unadulterated hogwash, but people are so insecure about having ideas on their own that they'll take anyone else's word over their personal knowledge and experience. Why else the proliferation of media pundits? Got your name on a book? You're an expert! It's better than buying a PhD diploma on the Internet. Trust me. Why do you think I wrote this book?

The idea that you can only change yourself flies in the face of reality. There is plenty of change that comes from the outside.

It is possible to teach even an old dog new tricks, and it doesn't have to take centuries of therapy; you just need a big enough stick. In other words, it requires the right kind of outside pressure. They've figured out how to make diamonds in less than a week in high-pressure vaults, and those gem stones are all but indistinguishable from the ones Mother Nature created by grinding away for millions of years. The same goes for human behavior.

Still, short of the right kind of external force, most people will take the easy way out every time. It's known as "the course of least resistance," and it works very well, thank you very much.

So, if you want to change the world, work to change others. It's too difficult to step outside of yourself, get objective, and then on top of it all, start changing yourself. Much too much work, and no fun. Much easier to recognize the problems of others and fix them.

This book then is a return to what most of us have been doing all along, more or less: trying to improve others. If we take charge by giving advice to them, surely—according to the law of "What goes around, comes around"—someone will take us on as a project. Which is what we've wanted all along, isn't it?

I recommend dispensing advice even if you'd never consider applying it to yourself.

After all, it is better to give than to receive. And that's biblical. You can look it up!

INTRODUCTION
Why Did I Write This Book?

If you're a reader who knows how to put two and two together, you can tell from my last name that I have a German background (the two ens at the end of Angermann are the giveaway). In fact, I grew up in Germany for my first 12 years and can claim bicultural status, although I've been a full-fledged American citizen for most of my life.

Now, Germans have certain peculiar qualities besides being rational, organized, reliable and orderly—they are born ready to line up in queues, for example. They have an internal clock so they're always on time (when they're late, it's on purpose). They are perfectionists. And they are thorough, some would say longwinded, long past the point where beating a dead horse is any fun. Ask a German, "How are you?" and he will tell you…for 45 minutes.

What most people don't realize is that beneath that orderly, rational veneer lurks a seething cauldron of anarchy. Think of it as the dark undercurrent of the German dream of perfection and total control, and when it comes bubbling to the surface, watch out! Organized chaos is a dangerous thing, as the history of the 20th century demonstrated with devastating results.

My Teutonic tendencies have been tempered, however, by 50 years of living in the Unites States. Americans, after all, like their chaos up front—preferably with guns blazing. They invented ultra-violence in movies and like to believe that having more weapons will actually make the world a safer place. Americans are also confused about freedom, liberty and opportunity, and individuality and conformity, which is why they express their uniqueness by living in gated communities where every house looks the same. But that's another story.

Since you're getting the best and worst of two cultures with me, it should come as no surprise that this book is both tendentious and to the point—plus occasional detours and excursions that you may ignore, if you wish, without missing any of the important stuff.

Which is why I will let you in on the big secret now: If you truly *get* the real 80/20 Rule on page 39, you can skip the rest of the book.

Unless you find my clever prose entertaining, in which case I suggest keeping this book in your bathroom and perusing it a chapter at a time, as needed. It may not be a cure for indigestion, but I do believe that it is as good an antidote for mental constipation as any, and the occasional chuckle may loosen you up in other satisfying ways as well.

Okay, 'fess up. Did you flip ahead to page 35 to sneak a peek? No?

Oh, go ahead! I'll wait. I'll even put a little space here with asterisks—a thought pause—before going on.

*****

Back already?

Okay, then. For those who still want to go the distance, let me spell things out.

When I turned 50, not only did I jump out of an airplane to make that birthday memorable (it was), but I also got to wondering if there was anything I knew for sure. After all, a half century of occupying space on this planet ought to add up to more than a few extra pounds in my midsection and the baby boomer mantra, "I'm still trying to figure out what to be when I grow up." At the same time, I was getting more and more pissed off at the unrelenting inanity and callousness of the folks that run our lives. But while fulminating about politicians or the absurdity of existence can be quite entertaining, it only goes so far.

Also, my son was entering his teenage years, and I wanted to have some fatherly advice for him. So I got to thinking, "What's the point of just flaming, complaining and heaping abuse on others? Shouldn't I offer a more positive message?"

I knew he wouldn't be interested in the great philosophies and theories of human behavior or the suffocating morality of most religions, which tell us how we should behave—all human evidence to the contrary—and take the fun out of life. What teenager is? What reasonable adult ought to be?

But might there not be some simple, easy-to-follow rules or principles on how to deal with life? Things I knew to be true *for sure*?

And why not give such advice? After all, it might save him years of going to shrinks, psychics and counselors, plus reading too many self-help books.

But we all know how well teenagers (and the rest of us) cotton to advice. So there has to be another, better way.

I call it messing with others for their own good.

In one of my former lives, I worked as a high school teacher in a public alternative school in New Haven, Connecticut. It was something like a magnet school before that term became popular. To my knowledge, we were the only public school in the United States that didn't have a principal. The superintendent tried to foist one on us every year—bureaucrats like to have control and tango with only one person in charge—but with the help of vocal parents, we, the faculty, managed to keep our independence. (It's amazing what a few shrill voices will do to the hypersensitive ears of school administrators.)

So, we didn't have a principal. Instead, a group of four teachers carried a reduced class load, which gave them the time to do administrative work and provide the necessary buffer between us and the higher ups. We called them the Facilitating Unit, or FU for short—I'm not making this up! As a result, we were able to develop our own curriculum, take "mental health" days as needed—yet have the lowest absentee rate of any group of teachers in the school system!—and felt that we actually had a say in how to educate our students. What a concept: giving teachers a real voice in the classroom, rather than forcing them to just make do in the face of the raging education debates!

This was important because our student population was diverse. It was not unusual to have the sons and daughters of Ivy League professors in the same courses as working-class Italian and Polish youngsters, ghettoized African-Americans and Hispanic adolescents, not to mention kids that could hot-wire any car in the city and had done serious time in juvenile detention. I met some of the smartest undereducated kids I have ever known at that school. They couldn't pass a math exam or read beyond the fourth-grade level, but they knew how to make change in their heads, figure out odds and read a situation for trouble faster than any of us on the faculty.

And it was the first time that I discovered the power of messing with others for their own good.

It happened when Alice Mick, one of the teachers, tried to clear a crowd of students from the basement of the school building, a favorite gathering place where kids from different ethnic and class backgrounds mingled in the course of buying, selling and smoking marijuana. Trying to disperse a horde of unruly students is never easy, especially when they're high, and she was having no success whatsoever. The rowdy kids thought it was great fun to grin and ignore her orders to leave. But then she hit upon an ingenious solution. She threatened to kiss them. Emptied the place in record time!

As a teacher, I quickly discovered that lecturing or rational discourse had little impact on my students. It was like telling toddlers to share their toys. They will only do so if you make them, and the lesson doesn't stick—in one ear, out the other. The only way I could have any effect was to stop them in their tracks, rearrange their universe, and let them experience things in a brave-new-world kind of way.

If you can produce that kind of bang, your students may not change, but they're more likely to remember…well, maybe not the subject matter, but certainly you, the teacher: "That Mr. Angermann, he's crazy!" High praise.

Since then, I have found that messing with others for their own good works just as well with adults.

Some of you who believe in the power of words might ask why traditional lecturing or straightforward advice doesn't work. The answer is quite simple. Most people don't listen; not because they can't hear, but because they're still teenagers at heart. When it comes to emotional development, most people, no matter what their age, operate at adolescent levels. If you think otherwise, just remember Bill Clinton and Monica Lewinsky when he was the most powerful man in the world. Or Anthony Weiner. Donald Trump is an exception: He's still in toddler mode.

Try telling a teenager something, anything, and you'll quickly discover futility. I know because I have a son who once was a teenager. I love him, but not for his attention span or the ability to listen to me. Plus, I remember my own teenage years when I knew everything better than everyone else, too. As Bob Dylan once wrote in a song, "Ah, but I was so much older then, I'm younger than that now."

As I have grown younger, I continue to be amazed that most adults don't really grow up all that much. When comes to the really important stuff—relationships, dealing with feelings, thinking about something creatively—they are actually no better than children. In many cases, worse; because they've lost any sense of wonder, curiosity or pleasure in discovering new things.

Don't believe me?

Just look at the infantile behavior of so many of our leaders, especially when they get caught with their proverbial pants down: "I never said that. I was misquoted. My words were taken out of context." Even when the video on YouTube says it all. How is that any different from a little kid caught with his hands in the cookie jar? "What cookie? Not me!"

Some may remember how upset Newt Gingrich got when he thought that President Clinton had snubbed him on a ride on Air Force One? He shut down the government because of the perceived slight! You think rational consideration had anything do with that? Or when Donald Trump goes on a Truth Social texting rampage? Or when the rest of our leaders in Washington let partisan politics upstage national interest every time? Don't tell me that's all clear-sighted, reasonable adult behavior.

Time to bring out the old Star Trek t-shirt that says, "Beam me up, Scotty, there's no intelligent life down here."

Nine out of ten people make emotional decision and then back them up with a slew of reasons (read: excuses). It's classic adolescent mode. At such moments there is no good way to talk to them. Their emotional attachments will trump rational thought every time.

Since a direct, reasoned approach doesn't work, the thing to do is to sneak up on people and upset their apple cart before they know what hit them and their natural resistance kicks in. You've got to blindside them, derail them from their usual tracks and aim them in a new direction. In other words, you've got to mess with them.

Besides, you can't mess with yourself for your own good—at least not in the sense I mean—any more than you can tickle yourself to make yourself laugh.

BASIC PRINCIPLES

In order to mess with others for their own good, there are certain fundamentals you should know:

People know less than they think.

Even experts and highly successful people are often so focused on one area of life—their bread and butter—that they are ignorant about the rest of the world. But success has inflated their ego like one of those balloons in the Macy's Thanksgiving Parade that they can't admit that to themselves. Hence, they are really quite vulnerable because they just don't realize how much they don't know. Important stuff, too, like how to raise their kids well, how to have a good marriage, or where to get the best pizza in the world.

On the other hand, the rest of us are no better or worse.

Remember shows like "Are You Smarter than a Fifth Grader," or when Leno was the host of "The Tonight Show," Jay-walking up to average Joes and Janes on the street and asking them simple questions they couldn't answer. Aside from their obvious entertainment value, they pointed out just how ignorant most people are. But laughing at them, or even with them, masks an important fact. The smarter, more brilliant and more articulate members of our species, the Albert Einsteins, Bill Gateses, Marilyn vos Savants and Neil deGrasse Tysons, are right there with the rest of us. They may know many things we don't, but there are just as many arenas where their ignorance and incompetence shine as brightly as the Friday night lights at a football game. Ask the right questions, and they'll dither, too, or will change the subject.

On the third hand, things always take longer than people think they will.

When you require someone to meet a quick deadline, you can count on them cutting corners along the way to the finish, which opens the door to problems you can exploit to mess with them. In one of my former lives, I was a professional theater director. Opening night is an absolute deadline—there is a paying audience—and you can't imagine some of the last-minute, behind-the-scenes quick fixes to get the show on the road. Without pins and needles and duct tape, these premieres would be a disaster. Well, life imitates art, but the consequences of screw-ups are more serious in the real world.

Finally, spending a lot of time and energy on something is no guarantee that the outcome will be great.

It takes as much time and energy to do a bad job as it does to accomplish a good one, to execute a good or bad design, to make a good or bad car. There are a lot of hamsters that think working the wheel furiously means progress.

Study these precepts and make them your own. They will allow you to mess with others at will.

DARE TO BE STUPID

The best advice I ever heard was about 45 years ago when I went to see a wonderful comedy group from San Francisco called "Duck's Breath Mystery Theater."

In the opening skit that night, a stodgy professor came out on stage to lecture his class—us, the audience. His message was: "Dare to be stupid"—or "Dare 2 b stupid," for those among you who like to text.

It was very funny and, of course, you had to be there. But there is no doubt in my mind: It was brilliant advice.

The Ducks haven't been together for quite some time, which is America's loss, but hopefully their advice will live on. By the way, around the same time, Weird Al Yankovic put out a record album with the same title. Must have been something in the air.

Dare to be stupid.

That's right.

Dare to be stupid.

I know it sounds silly and lightweight, but it works.

For example, you're listening to some guy in charge talk up a storm. Like the pointy-headed boss in the Dilbert cartoons, he's blowing just so much hot air, making little or no sense. Rather than sit there and nod your head like you're actually taking it all in, dare to be stupid. Raise your hand, smile and say, "Excuse me, could you explain this at the 101 level for dummies like me?"

It usually stops them in their tracks. You've just messed with them for their own good. After all, they think they're communicating. So they may be annoyed, but nine times out of ten, they will comply and adjust their presentation and bring it out of the clouds down to Earth, or at least to a level where the rest of us mortals can follow.

This works well with teachers and professors in seminars and workshops. Try it on your doctor the next time he or she laces a diagnosis with incomprehensible medical gobbledygook.

Often when I do this in public, people come up to me afterwards and thank me for speaking up. They tell me that they felt the same way I did, but were afraid to say anything because they did not want to look—that's right—stupid. See how easy it is to become a local hero?

But be careful. You don't want to preface your interjections with something like, "I'll dare to be stupid here. What did you mean by…?" That will have the opposite effect. People will think you're calling them stupid and get sour.

It is interesting that "stupid" is one of those words that still can get a rise out of a lot of guys. You can rag them on anything short of their mother and they'll be good-humored about it. But call them stupid and even the greatest moron on the face of the earth will feel insulted and upset enough to want to kick your ass.

Which is too bad, because it gives "dare to be stupid" a bad name when, in fact, it is one of life's great pleasures.

Anytime you have a problem, challenge or a difficult decision to make—you're on the fence about something and the pickets are poking up your you-know-what—here's what you do. Dare to be stupid. Do something, anything, anything at all. Your actions will provoke a reaction, and you'll be on the move. You'll be making progress. If it steers you off-course, you can correct it. And you'll feel better because you've gotten a move on!

Put "Dare to be stupid" on top of your to-do list. Practice it at least once a day. It takes very little effort, because it's so easy to accomplish.

If you make it your goal, you will achieve it in no time and leave your fingerprints all over the scenery.

The bottom line is: If you dare to be stupid, you will express yourself, for better and worse. And when you push against the universe, the universe will push back. It's a law of physics: for every action there is an equal and opposite reaction. It's true because it was discovered by Isaac Newton, the first Apple guy.

Dare to be stupid, and you will change the lives of others in ways you can't even begin to imagine.

And best of all, it won't cost you a dime. Remember, this is a free country, and therefore stupidity is free, too.

TRY ANYTHING TWICE

Often at a party or some other get-together, people ask me to sample some new, exotic food concoction or other. They usually come up to me with a look of apology, as if they were intruding on holy ground. It turns out that they feel awkward about recommending that others try new things. These folks clearly haven't mastered the art of daring to be stupid or messing with others for their own good.

Whenever they approach me that way, I say, "Sure, I'll try anything twice." And they always laugh, like I've made a clever joke.

Little do they know that I am dead serious.

We live in a herd mentality culture. For all the apparent emphasis on individuality and self-expression, most people are terrified of doing anything unfamiliar. When I lived in Brooklyn, New York, I was amazed to meet people who were born and raised there, but had never been to Manhattan, a mere subway ride away. Some of them had lived for more than 50 years in their neighborhood, but they had never crossed the Brooklyn Bridge to check out what was on the other side (although they were certain that evil lurked among the sky scrapers, and they wanted no part of it).

People move into residential "communities" in the burbs or certain retirement meccas in Florida and Arizona and accept draconian rules about what they can and can't do to their homes and yards, all in the name of keeping up property values. In one such community in Florida, the homeowners' association made one of the residents take the tiles off his brand-new roof, because they were a shade off the approved colors. Living in look-alike, ticky-tack McMansions provides proud homeowners with a sense of security. They feel safe and cozy in the comfort of the herd.

So when I say, "I'll try anything twice," it tickles the funny bone of people's insecurity about stepping out, and it puts them at ease for having suggested that I do so instead. And they laugh.

Little do they know that I am dead serious. (See? Anything twice. Anything!)

Here's why.

If you pay attention, life gets more interesting with repetition.

Try it. Read this book twice. What a concept!

See the same movie twice. You'll notice different things and, for all you know, it might improve your viewing pleasure.

Besides, it is impossible to get the full benefit of an experience in one try. There are too many variables. Plus, the next time, things often turn out differently. Now you have two truths to contend with. Which is a good thing. The more truths you have the better. (People who are not confused about the difference between truth and facts will know what I mean.)

Of course, it doesn't count if someone offers you white asparagus for the first time and you take two spears on your plate. You must let some time pass and refresh the palate, as wine tasters do, before the second try. And that goes for non-culinary experiences, too. Whether you decide to go skydiving, deep sea fishing, or taking a walk outside of your neighborhood.

In business, especially if you have a managerial job, it may take as long as two years before you understand all the important issues, because you'll have to go through the annual cycle *twice* to get all of the nuances. And to find out which results were accidental rather than due to honest effort.

As for marriage, earthquakes and hurricanes, once may be more than enough. On the third hand, more second and third marriages "take" than on the first go-around, which just proves my point.

Now, it is true that Heraclitus, the ancient Greek philosopher, said that you can't step into the same river twice—so the second time around is not just a repetition but actually a brand-new experience. But let's not get all philosophical here and debate the meaning of meaning. It may not be the same river, but it's still water, and if you dip your toe in, it'll get wet.

So make "I'll try anything twice," your motto. It will mess with the expectations of others and put a smile on the face of the people you grace with its wisdom.

MIND YOUR MANNERS

Everyone complains that the world has become a ruder place. Public discourse, political campaigns with their vicious attack ads, children misbehaving on the street....

Many theories have been advanced in explanation for this development—single parenthood that doesn't allow time for teaching kids how to act right, lax morality, violent and oversexed television, all-pervasive social media, the deterioration of Christian values, etc. Everyone seems to agree that things were better when Grandma and Grandpa grew up.

Some of these hand wringers and breast beaters just don't have a sense of history. At various times in the past, people were just as ugly and personally abusive as they are today. Watch a few episodes of HBO's *Deadwood*, and you'll hear just how crude, rude and foul-mouthed the citizens of mining towns were in the Old West. American politics has a fine tradition of slandering opponents. Thomas Jefferson hired a journalist to spread false rumors about John Adams, his rival for the presidency. In return, his opponents spread rumors (confirmed as true by DNA evidence 200 years later) about Jefferson's relationship with his black slave, Sally Hemings. It was LBJ (that's Lyndon Baines Johnson, our 36th president, for those of you too young to remember) who counseled a would-be Texas congressman behind in the polls during an election campaign to call his opponent a "pig fucker" and have him deny it.

But let's assume that there were periods of gentility and pockets of politeness in the history of our country. When everyone lived in one place and we all had extended families, it was aunts, uncles, grandparents and neighbors who would reinforce good values and the golden rule, and people grew up with good manners. Ah, the pleasures of looking with rose-colored hindsight back to the golden age! But I'm not really interested in harping on what caused the decline in civility since then. Or lamenting the fact that we can't go back to the good old days, which weren't all that they were cracked up to be anyway.

As one of my friends likes to say whenever someone utters the phrase, "It takes a village"—"In that case, I want to be the village idiot."

What I want to focus on is what to *do* about rude behavior: Stop moaning. Dare to be stupid. Do something for yourself and mess with others for their own good!

With children it's usually quite easy. Expectations and consistency work miracles. Most of the time, their acting out is just a way of screaming for boundaries. My wife and I discovered that whenever our son drove us up the wall with his behavior, it was because we were confused about how we wanted him to act. When we finally sat down and agreed on what *we* wanted, and treated him accordingly, the misbehavior disappeared within a week. (On occasion when that didn't work, we talked to other parents who had kids his age about how he was driving us nuts and were delighted to discover that they were having the same problems. Then we knew it was a phase our son would outgrow, and we could relax. It wasn't us being confused.)

With teenagers, you have to be more creative. Complaining, even hassling, will only get you so far. Remember the futility of rational discourse and advice.

When my son was an early adolescent, he went through a period of not flushing the toilet after he used it in the morning—he claimed he was too tired to do much more than stumble out of bed. I kept reminding, okay, nagging him, but my words had no effect whatsoever. I thought of putting up a sign above the commode that said, "Out of order. Your urinal taxes at work," but he wasn't that kind of contributing member of society yet, and I couldn't be sure he'd get the point. Plus, I was too lazy to go out and buy poster board and magic maker just to be a smart-aleck.

Then I had an idea. One night after he'd gone to bed, I got out a deck of cards, sneaked into the bathroom and spread out a winning poker hand on top of the porcelain water tank—a royal flush.

The next morning, I heard him get up, stagger into the bathroom and mumble to himself. A long pause…. Then, "Hey, Dad, what the… oh, oh, I get it!" The ensuing gurgle from the flushing toilet was music to my ears. Over the next few days, I varied the hand, just to keep him interested long enough to establish a new habit. Problem solved.

As for the rest of the world…it is up to you to let people know how you want to be treated.

Take those sales clerks at the checkout counter who should be ringing you up but get distracted by the ringing telephone instead. Immediately, they pick up and forget that you exist, answering queries and looking up information for someone at the other end. It is quite aggravating. And bad customer service. I wouldn't mind them picking up the phone and saying, "Please hold, I'm with a customer." But no, technology trumps the flesh-and-blood person in front of their nose every time. Before long, they'll ignore you until they've finished with their texting and tweeting.

So I have come to do the following. When they hang up and finally turn their attention back to me, I wait until they have rung up the sale and say, "I'm sorry, I changed my mind waiting while you were on the phone. I'm going to buy this item somewhere else, where the customer comes first."

Sometimes they apologize. More often than not, they snap into defensive mode. And that's okay. I don't expect people to get it. I just plant seeds. A few will sprout. Most won't. But that's never stopped a good farmer from sowing.

It helps to smile. After all, it's not really their fault. At the sales clerk level, it means they haven't been trained properly, which is the fault of the company, business owner or store manager.

The key to correcting the behavior of others is to do so calmly. The best way is to smile politely and put them on the spot. If you can't do it without getting angry, don't. People getting yelled at will only pick up on your emotion—anger, fury or frustration—and tune out everything else, including the meaning of your words. They'll apologize, but only to get you off their case. They won't understand that it's about them, because they will only register the intensity of your emotions and think that there is something wrong with you.

Another way to say this is—if you get angry, you're just letting the other asshole reduce you to his or her level, and you'll miss out on the opportunity to mess with them.

GO CRAZY

One night, when my wife and I were still living in New York City, we were heading home from a movie and heard the squeal of brakes and the ugly sound of one car impacting another. Turning the corner to our apartment block, we came upon the aftermath of a fender bender across the street. Apparently, one driver had started to pull out of his parking spot when the other came along and clipped his left front fender. The driver that was hit had gotten out of his car already and was yelling insults at the other guy. His whole body was shaking with fury as he escalated to ever more strident levels of hysteria.

A squad car pulled up on our side of the street and two policemen got out. One cop approached the culprit who was still sitting in his vehicle with the windows rolled up and, I imagine, the doors locked. The other, a big Irish-looking hulk, moseyed over to inspect the damage on the other car. He tut-tutted and ahemmed. Suddenly, without warning, he wheeled on hysterical owner and barked, "What the fuck's the matter with you! Get a grip!" His whole physicality changed from mild keeper of the peace to dangerous, unpredictable madman. The driver sobered up instantly. Without missing a beat, the policeman switched back to amiable-cop-in-uniform mode. He clucked in sympathy and nonchalantly continued examining the damage to the car—all in a day's work.

In movies the cop, played by someone like Bruce Willis, Harrison Ford or Liam Neeson, would probably have slapped the frantic guy, but this was a more elegant solution. He stopped him cold, like a great running back freezing a defender before continuing down the field to score a touchdown. He messed with the car owner big time for his own good. Being calm and attempting to reason with him in all likelihood would only have encouraged higher decibels of hysteria. Going crazy on the guy stopped him in his tracks.

No doubt, there are other ways of responding in such instances, but this is a useful tool for coping with extreme situation. Sometimes, you have to go nuts. It may save your life.

My dentist told me how he managed to get out of a serious scrape that way. When he was in dental school in downtown Chicago, he often took the El home after class late at night. One time, he was sitting alone waiting for the train when five young punks came up the stairs at the other end of the platform. Uh-oh. He saw them look in his direction, huddle for a moment and start to move toward him. He could tell that they spelled trouble (even if they weren't smart enough to read the sign across the platform).

Then he got inspired. As they came closer, he snorted, coughed, spit on the platform, poked his index finger up his nose, and started an elaborate ritual of "drilling for oil." He scrunched up his face and added slobbering, grunting sounds until the gang turned away in disgust. They didn't want to mess with a crazy guy or besmirch themselves with his snot. They never realized how thoroughly he had messed with them (albeit in this case, for his own good).

You can go crazy on people even when they're not in a state of crisis. Feel free to rattle them like an earthquake.

It's what great art does. Sure, some of it holds up a mirror we don't usually want to gaze into. But when it really takes off, it can shake us to the core of our being, make us see the world in new light and transform us.

TV SHOWS

If you want to see the process of messing with others for their own good in action, there are several fine television shows that make this practice part of their stories. Some are no longer on the air, but still eminently worth watching, and you can catch them on Netflix, Hulu, Amazon Prime, Acorn TV or other streaming websites:

Ted Lasso

NCIS

Still good after all these years., even without the inimitable Leroy Jethro Gibbs (Mark Harmon).

Being Erica

A young woman who gets to relive her most embarrassing moments and fix or accept them.

Any George Carlin comedy specials

Lots of clips available on YouTube. Never gets old.

Any of the "news" comedy or late night shows anchored by John Oliver, Jimmy Kimmel, Bill Maher, etc.

If you aren't a fan yet, I'll leave it to you to explore them on your own. If you are, you'll know what I'm talking about.

THE GOLDEN RULE REVISITED

Many of us are unhappy with the service we receive, be it in restaurants, theaters, banks or retail stores. We swallow rudeness and allow moronic behavior to pass without proper reward. On the way home, we get pissed off all over again, complain to our spouses or kids in the car, carp and cavil (two fine words worth adding to your arsenal of alliterative phrases), and run scenarios in our head on how to get even—none of which solves anything.

True, most people don't go out of their way to insult you. It's usually just ignorance or mediocrity on parade.

So it's up to you to apply corrective measures. And the best way to do this is to apply a wrinkle of the golden rule: "Do unto others as you would have them do unto you":

Teach others as you would like to have them do unto you.

Better yet: Mess with them.

Let me give you a few examples.

We've all had the experience of going to a restaurant, hoping for a pleasant, intimate experience with family, friends, a new date, or an old lover, and getting bothered by a hovering waiter. Not content with the one-time cruise-by, "How is everything?" he or she returns like the yo-yo from hell and keeps pestering you. "How's it going?" "Can I get you anything else?" and my all-time favorite, "May I take this from you, or are you still working on it?"

The way to deal with that last bit of idiocy isn't to yell, "No, you blithering nincompoop, I came here to eat! If it were work, I wouldn't bother!"

Instead, smile and say, "Yes, I am; but I don't seem to have the right tool. Could you get me a chisel or a hacksaw?" This works especially well if you still have a chunk of meat on your plate. At some point you'll see an "Aha" light bulb go on: Your waiter thinks he gets you—you're just kidding—what a card!

But he'll leave you alone. And he's likely to remember you next time, if you choose to patronize the establishment again.

By the way, I always tip fairly regardless, unless the service is truly atrocious. Again, the point is not to blame. Almost all waiters are mediocre at their job. It's that kind of occupation in the United States. In Europe, they actually have to go to school and pass an exam—it's a respected profession there, with standards—but here the only requirement seems to be showing up.

So I leave a tip. I consider 20% fair, more in the rare case that the waiter actually knows what he or she is doing. I drove a cab for six months once, and I know that a good tip can make your day.

Plus, if you stiff the servers, they'll just think you're a skinflint. They won't make the connection between your protest by omission and their mediocre behavior.

Here is another example.

No one seems to be teaching basic telephone etiquette to teenagers anymore. Probably because Millennials prefer texting which, as a visual medium, has different rules and codes of behavior. Still, most people have occasion to use the phone, even if they don't know what dialing is.

When my son reached middle school, he suddenly received phone calls from all kinds of female admirers and some new male friends he'd made. The phone would ring. I'd pick up and hear a voice demanding, "Is Erik there? Let me talk to him."

The first time I was so surprised, I actually did what I was told. The next time I decided to do something about it. When I heard, "Can I talk to Erik," without introduction, I replied, "Who is this?" And when the other party identified herself—in this case, Jennifer—I said in a friendly voice, "Hi, Jennifer, this is Erik's dad. When you call someone, you should identify yourself first and say, 'Hi, this is Jennifer. May I speak with Erik, please.' The next time you call, please do so."

And then I hung up.

Well!

Within two days my son came home in a tizzy. "Dad, what did you say to my friends. They're all afraid to call here."

I explained to him what had transpired and watched him roll his eyes as he left the room. But his friends, those brave souls that had the courage to call again, all said the right words, or some acceptable version thereof.

By the way, Jennifer was the only one who called back right away and followed my directions to a tee—which is probably why I remember her name. So I responded as effusively as I could, "Hello, Jennifer, it's good to hear from you. I'm sorry Erik is not home, but I will give him the message that you called. Please feel free to call back any time."

Credit American Express with introducing the proper way to end a telephone conversation with a customer. The company started the practice of finishing up by saying, "Is there something else I can help you with?" That leaves the decision with you, the caller. It was such an effective improvement that everyone else copied it. As a result, it has become commonplace for just about all customer service specialists (!) to bring conversations to a close that way. It's a good thing, and I am glad it has caught on industry-wide, even if it makes everyone sound like they've been cloned.

THE REAL 80/20 RULE

> *No one ever went broke underestimating the intelligence of the American people.*
> —H. L. Menken

In business there is something called Pareto's principle. It was named after a 19th-century economist who discovered that 20% of the population in Italy owned 80% of the land. Later it became known as the 80/20 rule and referred to the notion that in business 80% of activity and effort has nothing to do with the desired outcome. Only 20% of what people do actually produces results that affect the bottom line in a positive way.

Numerous self-help books have been written about this principle, and it has been expanded to other areas of people's lives—happiness, self-fulfillment, etc. The idea is to focus your attention on the 20% and not bother with the rest. You'll get a lot more done. Be a 20%er, and your life will improve beyond your wildest dreams.

This is all very well and good, but as with many other self-help notions, while the rule may be true and useful, it has had little impact on most people's lives. They still go around spinning their wheels and complain that there is not enough time in 24 hours to accomplish all they have to do.

The main reason why the rule has been ineffective is that the way it is usually explained and applied misses the point. There is a more fundamental meaning that no one ever talks about, a more powerful use; and if you really get this, it *will* change your life!

Here then, without embellishment or edification, is the real 80/20 rule:

In any human endeavor, activity, art, craft or profession, 80% of the people are mediocre.

This means, only 20% will look beyond the immediate solution, think out of the box, do more than expected, approach the situation with a sense of curiosity and bring a modicum of original thought to the table. The rest will just muddle along.

The rule hold true for judges, doctors, lawyers, soldiers, plumbers, electricians, home builders, teachers, parents, flower arrangers, tinkers, tailors and candlestick makers. Not to mention U.S. presidents, Catholic popes, and leaders of any other organization more than 100 years old.

Take professional sports. In basketball, for every Michael Jordan, Larry Bird, LeBron James, or Caitlin Clark, in their prime, who could elevate their play and take over a game at will, there are four other players on the team that can't. Even today, when the game has changed to emphasize 3-point shooting. Stephen Curry may be a brilliant player, but he could not dominate a game, like Kevin Durant, whose injury cost the Golden State Warriors the 2019 NBA Championship.

80/20—do the math.

I know there are sports fans who will object that the other team members are hardly mediocre ball players. After all, they represent the cream of athletes in their sport. I would agree. But relative to the superstars, they are definitely in a lesser league and demonstrate the 80/20 rule quite nicely.

In some professions the split is even more skewed toward mediocrity—in politics, the media and the film industry it's closer to 95/5. In the U.S. Post Office, too. If you've seen the number of clerks behind the counter get smaller as the line of customers gets longer, because they will take their break regardless of what's happening, you know what I'm talking about. But in most walks of life, 80/20 is a good rule of thumb.

There will be people upset by this. They don't like the word "mediocre" being applied to them. It offends their sensibility. They don't like "average" either, but they've dealt with that to their satisfaction. Like most car drivers, everyone thinks they're above average, so there! But what they're confused about is the difference between mediocrity and ordinariness.

Mediocrity arrived on the scene because of our mistaken belief what equality means in American society—that everyone can be anything they want to be and achieve greatness in any walk of life. This has led to an obsession with achievement, which requires discrimination and judgment: Once you cherish outstanding, extraordinary and exceptional accomplishments, you open the door to mediocre ones, too.

Ordinariness, on the other hand, is something that all human beings share equally—it doesn't take any special ability to be part of the human race. That is one of its glories. And something most people forget. There is no judgment involved. Recognizing and honoring the essential humanness of others is simply a matter of acknowledging that we're all struck from the same DNA, that we're all atoms and electrons dancing madly with some notion of consciousness, that we're all connected somehow.

If we could leave it there, we might be OK. But we also know that we've all got to die. And from the anxiety about our death—this is very Freudian—is born the need to be somebody. To contend. To achieve. To be better than the rest. Yet, it doesn't change anything about the fundamental human condition. Accepting that is hard. Easier to run, race, move quickly and judge ourselves superior to others.

Which brings us back to the 80/20 rule.

It may be a difficult idea to wrap your head around at first—that 80% of all practitioners of an activity or profession are mediocre—but it explains a lot of things.

Take politics. When 80% of the people believe what our elected leaders and their media shills tell them, without asking any questions—in other words, act like mediocre followers—and only 20% will take the time to learn and think about the issues, it's hardly an informed electorate that puts people into office. Why else would the approval rating of Congress be in the toilet, yet most U.S. Representatives get re-elected. Gerrymandered districts are only part of the problem. Most voters pick their leaders based on personality and the platitudes and promises they hear from them during the campaign. Then, they give them the benefit of the doubt until they really screw up. That's when they get mad—an emotional response—and in time, throw the bums out and elect someone else that promises them the moon.

Of course, when you have someone in a position of authority who surrounds himself with like-minded 80% cronies and mediocrities—some will remember Harriet Myers, George W. Bush's supreme court nominee, Attorney General Alberto Gonzales, and Michael Brown ("Brownie"), the head of FEMA during the Hurricane Katrina disaster?—you also get a cadre of people who do "a heck of a job" while the country goes to the dogs.

By the way, just because you're more comfortable around smart people, doesn't mean you'll escape the 80/20 rule, as President Obama found out after less than a year in office. A good number of his appointees quickly demonstrated their mediocrity—ex-Harvard president Larry Summers and Secretary of the Treasury Timothy Geitner. As for Obama himself—he was a 20%er when it came to running a campaign, but more of an 80%er governing, aloof and unwilling to wade in, sell his accomplishments, and do the work to make his programs succeed.

One of the worst things about the Trump administration is the president insisting on surrounding himself with people doing his bidding and unwilling to challenge him. The results are a mediocre cadre of White House and appointed government officials, although his press secrcretary, Karoline Levitt, is undeniably a 20%ers at prevarication.

Then there's the confusion we have about our sports and media heroes. We expect them to be in the 20% group in all aspects of their lives, just because they're gifted at threading a ball through a hoop, putting it into a hole or cracking it with a bat. And we are shocked, yes shocked, when they turn out to be mediocrities at everything else.

Michael Jordan, arguably the greatest basketball player ever, has been so-so at virtually everything else in his life. When he tried his hand at professional baseball and spent a year in the minors, he could never hit a curve ball better than an average utility player. He's an okay golfer. And in the rest of his endeavors? Well, he had an extramarital affair, which led to divorce, and had to settle with his ex-wife to the tune of $130 million, so his track record when it comes to relationships is not exactly stellar.

Another example was the media hoopla surrounding the revelations that Tiger Woods was a sex addict, not to mention his inept handling of his affairs, including the much televised *mea culpas* to his sponsors, fans and mother. He may have been a top 1% golfer then, but he was an 80%er in the rest of his life.

We expect perfection from our sports, media and political figures, and we tut-tut or gloat when we discover that they are lacking as spouses, parents, financial experts, etc., etc. Shame on us.

I'm not saying we should make allowances for people when they act like jerks; but please, let's show a little common sense. The ancient Greeks knew that people are imperfect and gave their heroes fatal flaws. Oedipus had his overreaching pride, Hercules was a muscle-bulging teenager with fits of uncontrollable rage—the Incredible

Hulk of his time—and the Olympian gods were philanderers of the worse sort. All that immortal power and might, and 80% for all the rest of their qualities.

Now, that doesn't mean that there is anything wrong with being an 80%er. If you have a cold or a simple bone fracture, any GP or orthopedic surgeon will do. But when you have a problem that isn't in the books or doesn't come with easily diagnosed symptoms, wouldn't you want a 20%er looking after you, someone like TV's Shawn Murphy, the "Good Doctor," or in an earlier show, Dr. House, who, regardless of his bedside manner, got excited by a challenge and thought creatively?

Once you get this principle, it makes life much easier. No longer will you need to get angry at incompetent professionals. No longer will you have a hernia if someone messes up at work. Or does a bad job tuning your car or fixing your plumbing. Or treats you for years in therapy and you're still unhappy and screwed up. Remember in a class of 200 medical students, the person who graduates at the bottom is called "doctor" the next day. And he'll have a diploma hanging in his office to prove it!

You'll understand that, as members of a vast tribe, it's not their fault. They're just mediocre at what they do. If you want better results, go and find someone exceptional. If you got burned in a messy divorce because your attorney was just a run-of-the-mill shark, hire a 20% barracuda the next time.

Understanding this principle also allows you to mess with others for their own good. Whenever people complain about their chiropractor, computer guru or financial analyst, I tell them, "Well, you know, 80% of the people in any profession are mediocre. Sounds like you got yourself one of those." That usually gives them pause, or stops their carping. At least with me.

THE REAL 80/20 RULE PART II

Now, there will be many who'll accuse me of being an elitist, anti-democratic, condescending curmudgeon. It's a mantle I wear with pride. Most Americans are confused about democracy and our founding fathers' and framers' wisdom. They think that "all men are created equal" means everyone can have everything they want, like many silly parents who want their children to believe that they can be anything they want to be.

Well, tell that to the 5' 4" basketball player dreaming of starring in the NBA. I had a friend in junior high school, who made Dr. J (that's Julius Erving, the man who invented playing the game above the rim) look like a spastic stick figure. He could fake anyone out of his jock strap and score at will. But he didn't grow taller, and by high school all the other players had shot up past him like so many beanstalks, and his interscholastic basketball career was over. He took up golf and became quite good at the game, but he never dominated the links the way he could the hoops.

What our founders really meant by "all men are created equal" was that everyone has equal opportunity to make their way in the world—or should have. But even that is a grand dream, since what family you're born into and where you live make an enormous difference in the future success of most people, especially when it comes to money and wealth. The glory of our system is that it provides *some* people with the chance to leave their background behind, and it makes no difference where they're from. But the exceptions do not prove the rule—that most people can't.

The myth that you can be anything you want to be dies hard. At the same time, while most folks prefer being part of the herd, the idea that it also means they're mediocre 80%ers doesn't sit well with them. Just about everyone in the world is a legend in their own mind.

But what really troubles their grey matter and inflated egos is the corollary of the 80/20 rule:

100% of the people are mediocre at what they do at least 80% of the time.

That should give pause to those who think themselves as superior to the rest of humanity. A little humble pie is never a bad thing.

My recommendation: Just accept it. After all, if you look at yourself without rose-colored glasses, you'll see all the areas in your life where you don't shine, either due to lack of motivation or lack of ability. Why beat yourself up because of the hand genetics dealt you? Spend your time looking for what you're really good at.

One of the great tragedies of life occurs when people desperately want to be in that 20% group but just don't have the talent. They will beat their heads against the wall for a long time and live unfulfilled lives. In some cases, they may even succeed in it as a career—many no-talent actors become movie stars anyway—but it won't make a difference. All the fame and money don't make up for the fact that deep down they want it to do something else for them, to validate them in a way their mediocre 80% performances and stardom never can. It's one of the things that keeps the Betty Ford Center in business.

I applaud *American Idol*. I don't watch the show or its spin-offs because I find them insipid and the fantasy of becoming a singing star doesn't tootle my flute. But *Idol* has, more than any other television program, given mediocre, no-talent wannabees the opportunity to get the pipe dream of musical stardom out of their system once and for all, thus sparing them years of wasted effort pounding the pavement without success in Nashville, Austin, New York and L.A. In fact, it has freed them to start looking in other places for their true gifts.

A different tragedy might occur when you are in the 20% group, but don't care a flea fart about it. Helicopter moms and other yentas may tut-tut, "But she's so talented!" So what? It doesn't matter if you're a brilliant musician or doctor, or an elite tennis player like Andre Agassi in his prime, if your heart's not in it. You may do it for some time, even become great, but you'll also resent it. On the positive side, when you retire, you may be financially set for life. Better yet, you may decide to get out early. For many, that's what their mid-life crisis is all about.

I discovered that in my 20s when I was teaching high school. After three years, I started to actually get good it—I had a knack for discovering how little my students really knew and pitching what I wanted them to learn in such a way that many actually got it. But I also knew my heart wasn't in it.

Fortunately, I complained about it to a friend late one night when we were sitting at the kitchen table shooting the breeze. After listening to me being existential and morose for much too long, she asked out of the blue, "What do you really want to do?" Without thinking, I blurted out, "I want to direct plays."

Oh boy!

There it was, lying on the table like an unwelcome gift. I couldn't return it or act like it didn't belong to me and didn't mean anything. It was either deny it, or go for it. I swallowed hard and decided to embrace it, and became a theater director for the next 20 some years. And I'm glad I did.

Be happy when such moments occur and surprise you. It is your true self speaking from deep within you with childlike simplicity and certainty. Be sure to listen to yourself then. It can save you a lot of time. At that moment, you have a choice—follow your passion, or turn your back on it. If you do the latter, you will be much more miserable than if you say "Yes." Time will tell if you are 20%er on that boardwalk of life or part of the mediocre crowd.

Yet another kind of tragedy can occur if you're a 20%er in something that our materialistic society doesn't value. "Do what you love and the money will follow" is another one of those idiotic saws inflicted on the American psyche. Of course, you must love what you do to feel satisfied, but it won't necessarily translate into cash or let you earn your keep. Think about poets—those rare birds who are really good with words. They may eke out a living with grants and teaching gigs, but they will never be J. K. Rowling, Bill Gates or Warren Buffett.

Why is this important?

If it is true that we all have divinity inside us, and our purpose on this planet is to grow, develop to our fullest capacity, and express our selves—be all that we can be, whether we join the Army or not—then pursuing an unfulfilling career may put bread, butter and bacon on the table, but it won't feed our soul.

Fortunately, there are a gazillion things you can do as a 20%er—cooking, parenting, sports, quilting, gardening, writing jokes, you name it. Lots of medical doctors are fine musicians, poets and photographers in their own right and have made their peace with pursuing their true giftedness as an avocation.

On the third hand, there are those individuals that like something so much it doesn't matter to them if they're any good at it or not. Albert Einstein, surely a 1%er when it came to astrophysics, was a mediocre violinist, but that didn't prevent him from fiddling for most of his life with unabashed pleasure.

MIND YOUR MANNERS—II

Don't you just love it when you're in a restaurant or at the supermarket and there are small children racing around, crying, pitching a temper tantrum and making an all-around nuisance of themselves? And the adults who should be curbing their misbehavior are either helpless or actually smile with pride, doting on their offspring.

I applaud the restaurants that attempt to deal with this problem by putting up a sign that says, "If we find your children running around unattended, we will gift them with 2 cups of cappuccino and a puppy."

But for those eating establishments that don't display such cleverness, it's up to you. Rather than smoldering and thinking hateful thoughts about the parents and their noisy little monsters, do something. If these folks believe their little prince or princess should be able to run around like the bulls at Pamplona, it's not just their problem. It's yours, too.

And don't assume any of them know what they're doing— remember the real 80/20 rule. It holds for parents as well. Mediocrity is a fact of life everywhere.

What I do in such situations is: I intervene. If the kids are dashing about, I shout, "Whoa! Time out! Time to slow down!" If they're yelling and screaming, I insist, "Turn down the volume, please."

Sometimes, if a child is on a crying jag but old enough to understand words, I will hunker down and ask, "What's your name?" That, and a strange, friendly face in front of their nose, distracts most children enough and gets them to think about something else. By the time they realize it, they've usually forgotten what they were crying about.

Many parents get it right away. They know their child was out of control and "screaming for boundaries." Maybe they weren't paying attention, in which case they'll wade in with an apologetic look and take over.

The ones that don't know any better, or actually think their kids should have the freedom to inflict themselves on the world in whatever manner they please—well, that's what you're there for. To intercede and, if necessary, mess with them for their and their children's own good.

The key is to remain calm, friendly and polite. If a parent objects to me interfering, I smile and say, "I'm only trying to make sure he (or she) doesn't hurt himself (or herself)."

When a mom or dad starts whaling away at a child in the aisles of a supermarket, I intervene and say, "Excuse me, there is no need for an adult to hit a small, helpless child in public."

If they say, "That's none of your business," I respond, "Oh, but it is—you made it my business. You see, it offends me to see big, powerful people beat up on someone less than half their size."

Always match their verbal intensity. Don't let them intimidate you. If they try to get on their high horse with you and exclaim, "How dare you…!" saddle up yourself and yell right back, "How dare you allow your children to bother me and the rest of the patrons in this restaurant. If you were smoking here, I would ask you to stop. I'm merely reminding your children of proper etiquette in public."

I could say, "how to act right in public," but "proper etiquette" will give them pause, because they don't really know what it means and probably have to think about it.

If they get annoyed and leave, let them. Good riddance. The patrons will applaud you. Some restaurant owners may even treat you for dinner.

If you encounter a bully who tries to threaten you physically to save face, I recommend saying, "I'm sure you can beat the crap out of me, but I'll bleed all over you, and *then* I'll have you arrested for assault." *

If that doesn't work, run. You're dealing with a psychopath—yes, they go to restaurants, too—and they don't care how much it hurts them, so long as they can hurt you.

---

* When I first wrote this book, the United States had a gun violence problem, but not to the degree it does now. These days the number of angry individuals acting out their frustration with weapons in hand has reached epidemic proportions. Add to that the efforts of some conservative state governors and legislatures to enact laws permitting anyone to carry a concealed gun without permit or training, and any irate encounter has the potential of turning into a bloody nightmare. While I don't think most people will go to such extremes in front of their children, you never know. So, I would counsel caution and recommend deescalating tense situations whenever possible.

THE REAL 80/20 RULE—III

I have mentioned parents in relation to the real 80/20 rule. No doubt that will rub some the wrong way. But it's true. Those who educate children—parents and teachers—unfortunately are as much subject to the iron-clad consequences of the rule as everyone else.

With teachers, there are historical reasons. Unlike other countries, where they are engaged in a highly esteemed profession, here in the United States, teachers command little respect. This attitude is best expressed by the cliché, "Those who can, do; those who can't, teach." Brutal, but not all that wrong. Like any old proverb or stereotype—love is blind, Scots are misers, Hispanics are temperamental—it contains more than a kernel of truth. But that is not the point. The tragedy is that we give our children, our most precious lifeblood, to a bunch of mediocrities for six or more hours a day.

Teachers are finally earning enough in some states to attract higher quality candidates. When I was in high school, all the male teachers had to take summer jobs because a teaching salary would not support their family. My junior year American History teacher, one of the 20%ers in his profession, drove a milk truck. (This was before it took two or more people in a household going to work to make ends meet.)

Most people will have little problem with the 80/20 rule applied to teachers. After all, who hasn't endured some dodo, fossil or eccentric character straight out of Charles Dickens at some point in their education. My fourth-grade teacher tried to scare us into acting right—behaving the way he wanted us to—by threatening to jump out of the second story window. It didn't work. We secretly cheered him on.

But parents? I can already hear the complaints. I'm being unreasonable. Worse yet, how dare I question the all-American notion that parents are uniquely qualified to know what's best for their kids. And do a heck of a job raising them to be responsible adults.

But is that really true? There is enough evidence about child abuse, incest, and absentee fathers and mothers to suggest that just because someone has the ability to engender or give birth to a child, he or she does not an ideal parent make.

Go to any athletic event for children and watch parents scream bloody murder at their little would-be soccer, basketball and football stars because their performance doesn't measure up to their own inflated egos and needs. In one high school ice hockey conference it got so bad the league banned the parents of one team from all games! Great role models there, and a completely wrong-headed notion of what sports for their kids should be about.

An orthopedist told me that he often has the parents of high school athletes ask him to prescribe steroids and other performance-enhancing drugs for their kids. He always refuses to do so, but he knows it's in vain. They will simply seek out another physician who is more amenable to their request. Surely, those parents don't know what is best for their children, even if they think they have their best interests at heart.

A college friend of mine refused to major in pre-med as his parents wanted him to. His father officially disowned him and put a notice in the local paper that he was no longer responsible for any and all aspects of his son's life. They did not speak to one another for two years before they made overtures to mend fences.

But I'm not just talking about such extreme cases. I'm referring to the vast swarm of Helicopter and Bulldozer parents and well-intentioned folks who believe that the fact that they love their kids and make sacrifices for them qualifies them as super moms and dads. Yet they are adequate parents at best—and according to the

80/20 rule, mediocre.

I'm not suggesting that others will do a better job, or that we should give parenting over to our government—God forbid! But let's not sugarcoat reality either.

Why else would there be so many depressed people, so many emotionally wounded birds, so many super-achievers who never feel they are enough, so many drug and alcohol users and abusers? Remember Hillman, "We've had a hundred years of therapy and the world's getting worse." Scratch the surface of civilization and its discontents, and you're likely to find an unhappy childhood lurking in the background, and no one really knows how to fix that.

Let me be clear, once again: This is not about blame. In most cases, I repeat, parents and teachers *do the best they can.*

Much bad parenting comes from ignorance and lack of experience. In the good old days, when there were communities and neighborhoods and extended families, collective experience made up for a lot of what was missing. Aunts and uncles disciplined their nieces and nephews. Grandparents could step in and tell young parents when they were overreacting.

But with nuclear families and one-parent households, stressed by financial woes, where is the safety net?

The good news is that motivated parents can improve. Given that mediocrity is the norm, it doesn't require much effort to raise the standard from "not okay" to "so-so." Plus, kids are resilient. It doesn't take genius parents to produce decent offspring. As education columnist John Rosmund said at a conference my wife and I attended "Parenting is easy. Marriage is hard. You can't tell your wife, 'Go to your room!'"

In the meantime, telling fathers and mothers that 80% of all parents are mediocre is one of the coolest ways to mess with them. Most people get flustered right away and take it personally—you know who they are! I often quickly add, "Of course, I'm not talking about you. But there should be tests that people who want kids have to pass first. They should have to get a parent's license, just like a driver's license."

It can be quite liberating to acknowledge that our mother or father may have loved us, but wasn't particularly good at raising us; that our parents did the best they could, but that their best was, yes, mediocre.

A good friend told me about a realization he had in his 40s. "You know, Chris," he said, "I've figured out that my mother isn't very smart." It was a liberating epiphany, which put a lot of his upbringing into perspective and allowed him to let go of some bad karma.

There is a caveat in all of this. Many people use a bad childhood as an excuse. In our victim-oriented culture, it has become a favorite American pastime. But the real implication of the 80/20 rule for all those blaming their childhood on their problems is this: They may be right, but what good does it do them?

I usually mess with people who complain about their upbringing by saying, "So you had a mediocre father (or mother). What are you going to do about it?"

MOVIES

Three great movies about messing with others for their own good:

The Karate Kid

"Wax on, wax off." The original flick with Ralph Macchio and Pat Morita is the one to get. Much better than the remake with Jackie Chan.

The King's Speech

The 2010 Oscar winner for best actor and best picture, and well deserving all the accolades and awards it got.

Frankie Go Boom

A hilarious, shaggy dog film (with a pig) starring Chris O'Dowd, Ronald Perlman, Lizzy Caplan, and Chris Noth.

MIND THAT ADJECTIVE

Considering the way our news media, politicians, family value advocates, far-left liberal lunatics and religious right ideologues abuse the English language, it is no wonder that most people don't know how to think for themselves. It's one thing for a comedian like Steven Colbert to fracture American-speak to make you laugh and think at the same time. It's another when people who should know better spew thoughtless nonsense. And it is nauseating when ideologues on the left and right, spindle, bend and mutilate usage to further their ends.

I first caught on to this a few years back when watching the way the media referred to people caught in the vicinity of some newsworthy disaster. The reporters would swarm like a bee hive on steroids to find some eye witness to interview. The caption running underneath often said, "Innocent bystander," or better yet, if they could get them on camera, "Innocent victim."

Then I started to wonder: Where are the *guilty* bystanders? The *reprehensible* victims? How come they didn't interview them? Couldn't find any? Or could it be that there weren't any? You get the point. When something significant or life-threatening occurs in your presence, you're either a bystander or a participant. Guilt or innocence has nothing to do with it.

Words determine how we see and experience the world. The stuff that gets fed into our minds and unconscious affects the way we deal with reality. Foolish, wrong-headed and redundant formulations add to mental clutter and encourage fuzzy thinking. People have gone to war for less.

That's why politicians and special interest groups spend so much time maneuvering to "frame" the debate. It matters whether we use "abortion" vs. "pro-choice," "troop surge" vs. "escalation," or "death panels" vs. "managed health care." Or when Fox News, one of the most biased networks on the airwaves, claims to be "fair and balanced."

The guy who first analyzed this phenomenon was George Orwell, the British writer, in his two visionary novels, *1984* and *Animal Farm*, and in his essay, "Politics and the English Language." He called it double-speak because he knew the truth of what Joseph Goebbels, the Nazi minister of propaganda, said about crowd manipulation: "If you tell a lie big enough and keep repeating it, people will eventually come to believe it."

Sounds like many of our current politicians and leaders, doesn't it?

The hall of politics, government and the military have been littered with Orwellian double-speak and bamboozling nonsense for some time, with phrases like "compassionate conservative," "collateral damage," and "friendly fire." More recent examples include, "true hero," "true genius," "intelligent design," and "fake news."

More often than not, such usages are an effort to deflect the true horror or meaning of an event or issue, to soften and dilute its impact. As we accept the terms uncritically, we stop thinking about them and no longer feel anything genuine in response.

Take the phrase "friendly fire" to describe someone being killed mistakenly by one's own fellow soldiers, companions or superior officers. Whoever came up with this doozy should be exposed to a dose of it himself, so he can experience just how friendly it is. It makes a horrific event sound like a birthday party rather than what it is—a terrible, deadly mistake.

What is needed is a simple means to separate clear-minded speakers and writers from the sloppy thinkers, obfuscators and manipulators, or just plain ordinary idiots. It happens I have just the tool for the job. I call it "Mind That Adjective," the perfect antidote to the gibberish that goes for meaningful discourse these days.

The way it works is: When you hear a phrase with an adjective, think of the opposite. If it makes sense, fine. If it doesn't, then the original phrase is likely to be nonsense, too.

Take the recent, "He's a true patriot," or "he's a true hero." Ever wondered what a false hero or ungenuine patriot would look like? The unnecessary exaggeration suggests that the speaker is either a card-carrying member of the Department of Redundancy Department or a sloppy thinker.

I remember when "intelligent design" first made headlines. I knew that it was a sham right away. Has anyone ever heard of unintelligent or downright dumb design on purpose? Would a watchmaker deliberately create a bad watch? Or an architect put up a bridge so it will fall down? Okay, American car makers invented something called "planned obsolescence" that would have cars break down sooner than necessary to encourage us to buy automobiles more frequently, but that's another story from another time

Seriously, no one sets out to make a lemon or a turkey when engineering something. So "unintelligent design," is a meaningless concept, which means "intelligent design" is too. And that's what it is—just another phrase shilling for creationism.

The way you can use "Mind That Adjective" to mess with others is to point out the discrepancy in their utterances. The next time someone waxes poetically about "this unfortunate tragedy," ask him if he has ever seen someone yuk it up after a tornado devastated their home. Or chime in sanctimoniously, "They are so blessed to experience this tragedy. They will surely use it as a learning opportunity to grow and develop their higher faculties."

THAT'S JUST YOUR OPINION

One of the easiest ways to get people's goat and raise their blood pressure is to counter their argument with the statement, "That's just your opinion." It's right up there with the insipid "Let's agree to disagree" for people who are uncomfortable with conflict or find themselves on the losing end of a good dispute.

"That's just your opinion" is a brilliant deflection. In one simple phrase you have

1. stated the obvious, and
2. invalidated everything your opponent has said up to that point.

Indeed, you have emasculated him or her—translation: cut off their balls (I include women here. I still remember the days when some of them said, "Don't break my balls," with a straight face).

But saying "That's just your opinion," is actually the refuge of lame-brained thinkers. Note how many people use it when they run out of ideas on how to respond to an elegantly formulated argument. This is equivalent to the "it's just a theory" argument against Evolution by evangelical ignoramuses; to which the proper response is, "So is gravity. Why don't you try jumping out of an airplane without a parachute and see what happens?"

Here's the way to deal with people who are too feeble-minded to meet your arguments head-on with a legitimate response:

When you hear, "That's just your opinion," respond, "Of course, it's my opinion. That goes without saying." (You have just called your antagonist an idiot.)

Then follow up with, "And it happens to be right!" Or, "It happens to be true!"

This brings the matter right back to where you were before your opponent tried to derail your line of reasoning. Only now you've taken the wind out of his sails, because he won't have a good follow-up.

At this point, most nitwits will opt for repetition, offering "That's just your opinion" once more.

To which the appropriate response is, "There must be an echo in here."

If they still persist, I suggest saying, "You are really emotionally attached to your point of view, aren't you?"

Now you've turned the tables. They may deny, bluster or bloviate—further evidence that you are right. But you've also given them the opportunity to realize how over-invested they are in their point of view. They may not admit it to you right then and there, but they might reconsider when they've had a chance to become more rational again. (One can always hope.)

Of course, there are lots of people who are incapable of rational thought, and it's best to avoid getting into an argument with them. I suggest saying, "I can't agree with you because then we'd both be wrong."

And extricate yourself as quickly as possible and move on.

SCREW-UPS

Apologize—to lay the foundation for future offense
—Ambrose Bierce

I'm sorry.
I apologize.
Oops.
My bad.

Apologizing for one's transgressions or demanding that others apologize for the ugly and foolish things they've done is useless. It's really just an excuse—the favorite tool of people in trouble to deflect serious repercussions for their mistakes and misdeeds.

Actually, "Oops, my bad," is almost okay because it acknowledges that a screw up has taken place. But most people say it like a shrug, not expecting to be called on the carpet for what they've done.

My favorite used to be politicians or leaders of failed companies saying, "I take full responsibility…" It's usually an attempt to turn aside calls for their resignation, hoping the storm of public outrage will blow over. None of them ever say, "It happened on my watch, it's my fault and I accept the consequences, so I will step down; or wear a hair shirt and have myself flogged three times a day for the next two weeks."

As if the shame of having to publicly admit that they or someone in their organization screwed up were punishment enough. This is the chest-bearing, *mea culpa* defense.

Some high-profile examples include Tiger Woods, the CEOs of Toyota and BP testifying before the U.S. Congress about separate screw-ups, and the growing number of peccadillo-addled politicians, starting with Twitter (now X) afficionado, Anthony Weiner, who lied on national television about his shenanigans, then "took responsibility" for it all, but resisted calls for his resignation for more than a week before giving in to the inevitable and bowing out. (Of course, his misbehavior pales by comparison with our current maniac texter-in-chief.) By the time this goes to print, we'll have been treated to further flagrant examples of hypocritical apologists from the sorry ranks of our politicians, athletes and media stars.

Gone are the days when taking responsibility for failure meant falling on one's sword, as Roman generals did after losing a battle, or at least cutting off the joint of a finger, which the Yakusa, the Japanese Mafia, demanded of its members after an egregious mistake.

The fact that apologies have become all but meaningless is demonstrated by the fact that the words, "I'm sorry," no longer carry enough weight, so in recent years, they've been replaced with "I'm soooo sorry." You can be sure when that no longer satisfies, we'll get even lengthier "sooooo's," the way razor companies keep adding more blades (as of this writing, we're up to five) to convince us that they will give a better shave.

When people apologize, hoping that their words of rue will make you or that the problem they've caused goes away, don't give them that satisfaction. Don't let them off the hook.

Here's what to do instead. When someone says, "I'm sorry," reply, "Okay, let's assume I accept your apology. What are you going to do about it? And 'I won't do it again' isn't good enough."

This is your best way of insisting that there must be consequences for the action—verbal or physical.

On the third hand, don't you apologize either.

Leroy Jethro Gibbs, the crusty veteran team leader on *NCIS* has a rule, "Never apologize. It's a sign of weakness." But that's a defensive posture. Plus, not apologizing has gotten a bad rep because

Donald Trump before he became president and since, has refused to admit to any blunders and mistakes while stonewalling his way past a multitude of embarrassments and crimes.

But such negative examples don't make saying "Sorry" any more legitimate than a slate of mediocrities running for office in most elections is a justifiable reason for not exercising one's right to vote.

The thing to do, instead of apologizing, is to acknowledge your screw ups.

Better to say, "You're right. I messed up. What do you want me to do?" That puts the ball squarely back in the court of the aggrieved party, where it has been all along. It asks them to deal with what happened in a positive manner, leads to negotiation and keeps channels of communication open.

Don't say, "What do you want me to do *about it*?" In most cases, there's nothing that can be done to undo or ameliorate the damage. You can't take back hurtful words or make anyone believe that you're not a racist, a sexist, an anti-Semite like Mel Gibson, or a blithering idiot like so many of our fearless leaders. If there is physical damage, it will have to heal on its own, or there will need to be some clearing away of the debris and serious rebuilding going on, just like after a tornado or hurricane.

If after you've said, "What do you want me to do?" the wronged person replies, "I want you to apologize," or "You owe me an apology," go ahead and be glad. If that's all it takes to wipe the slate clean for the offended party, say it with as much seriousness and contrition as you can muster—in other words, say it like you really mean it.

And heave a quiet sigh of relief that you got off so easy and with so little consequence.

CELEBRATE STEREOTYPES

In our era of political correctness and extreme wokeness, stereotypes have gotten a bad rap. It's OK to make fun of your own gender and ethnic subgroup in a self-deprecating way, but woe to those who joke about their ethnic neighbors or people of other religious affiliations. If you're in a profession with a high public profile, such a guffaw can be a death sentence.

Some extremists on the subject have gone so far as to claim that men cannot write believable female characters, or that only blacks can comment on the African-American experience.

In Europe and other parts of the world, they're not quite as silly yet as in the United States (although they import many of our mediocre practices and products, like McDonalds hamburgers). Part of the reason is that different folks have been living there next to each other and frequently beating up on one another for thousands of years, so history and first-hand experiences have taught them that cultural differences are real and matter.

They also understand that stereotypes address general behavior and don't hold true for individuals. It goes without saying, for example, that some women are physically stronger than many men, yet on the whole, the male gender is clearly more muscular and physically powerful. This is an easy one, since it is biologically and genetically based.

But cultural differences are just as deeply rooted and significant. And they derive much of their power from the fact that they are deeply unconscious for most people. Which is why comedians can make their living pointing them out and making fun of them.

The American anthropologist Edward C. Hall did seminal studies about the different perceptions of space and time of American,

German, French, Japanese and Arab cultures. During the 1950s, he worked at the U.S. State Department to teach intercultural communication to American diplomats, although from our track record you wouldn't think he made much of an impression. But that doesn't invalidate his findings.

Germans, for example, relate to space in a seemingly peculiar way. During World War II, when Americans housed German prisoners of war in Texas, Colorado and Florida in barracks, four to a room, they were in for a surprise. The Germans divided up their cramped, living quarters with blankets hung from wires and ropes they'd strung across the room, and each took one tiny, private area for himself.

That is because Germans extend the boundaries of their bodies to the edges of the room or house they occupy in an almost physical way. It's why they have doors with handles even on kitchens, and keep them closed. They feel better if you knock and give them the opportunity to invite you into their space, rather than having you barge in, which they experience as you crowding their liver and spleen.

I once tried to mediate an argument between a couple who got into a major tiff whenever the American-born wife brought her German-born husband's dry cleaning home and hung it up in his closet, paying no attention to where it ended up on the coat rack. I tried to explain to her that it made him feel like she was invading his body and rearranging his organs, but she thought I was nuts. She didn't notice her husband nodding vigorously in the background.

Knowing such culturally based patterns allows you to mess with others. Take, for example, the fact that northern Europeans—Norwegians, Swedes, Danes, Dutch and Germans—need a greater personal distance from others to feel at ease than folks from Mediterranean countries—France, Spain, Italy and Greece. People from southern climates have lived more densely packed for millennia and feel comfortable with, nay, even prefer closer distances to others than their cousins north of the Alps.

These differences have been imported into our American culture. Swedes from Minneapolis will prefer holding conversations farther apart than Italians from New York or Philadelphia. Try it at a party. If you invade someone's comfort zone, they'll draw back. If you're too far away, they will close the gap. You can lead someone across the room that way without their ever knowing what's going on.

The problem develops when stereotypes turn negative or are used to make fun of people maliciously. I'm not talking about Henny Youngman's hilarious, equal-opportunity-offending one-liners about various national and ethnic groups. They just point out the power and truth of stereotypes.

But while I can understand people reacting negatively to ethnic or sexist slurs with a vengeance, the pendulum has swung too far. Political correctness nowadays insists on a holier-than-thou approach that wishes to eliminate all stereotypes, diminishing our understanding of what makes people tick.

Plus, it makes the world a duller, sterner, grayer place, and it will make it harder to mess with people for their own good. It reminds me of Bertolt Brecht's play "Galileo," where one of the disciples of the great Italian scientist laments, "Pity the country that has no sense of humor."

BOOKS

In this brave new digital world, it is likely that "brick and mortar" books will no longer be the primary way information is disseminated (although the process of creative writing, andorganizing one's thoughts in a linear way—without relying on AI—won't change). Still, there are some fine historical examples of novels that tell stories and have messing with others for their own good as part of their makeup.

> *Catch-22* by Joseph Heller
>
> *Fear and Loathing in Las Vegas* by Hunter S. Thompson
>
> *The Once and Future King* by T. H. White
>
> *The Screwtape Letters* by C. S. Lewis (the Narnia guy)

In fact, any good narrative, TV show or movie messes with others for their own good. The point is to keep the reader or viewer engaged, surprised and entertained. That's why writers use all kinds of tricks to mislead—mess with—their audiences to heighten the pleasure of the experience and outcome.

Good comedians do it, too. A well-told joke produces anywhere from a groan to a chuckle to a barrel laugh. What better way to mess with others for their own good than to make them lose control for a moment and up their endorphin count.

Remember, it takes more than 40 muscles to frown, but only 10 to say, "Fuck you!"

LEADERSHIP

Speaking of books, it's a good thing that the American public's interest in printed matter on leadership has waned. Apparently, people no longer hang on every word of a winning football or basketball coach who wants to draw parallels between life and the gridiron field or hoop arena.

I am glad. For too many years, "leadership" was a favorite buzz word for the self-help crowd. The spate of advice books on how to go to the head of the pack—developing the leader within you, finding the leader inside, learning the 21 laws of leadership—all struck me as a bit silly. Did we really think the leadership principles of anyone historically memorable, from Jesus to Abraham Lincoln to Genghis Khan, would hold water in the 21st century?

Or that the winning principles of someone capable of inspiring elite athletes would offer a valuable blueprint for the rest of our lives? Take the famous quote attributed to legendary Green Bay Packer coach Vince Lombardi (although he never actually said it): "Winning isn't everything, it's the only thing." Apply that one to your marriage or relationship with your children, and see where it gets you!

Anyone with the slightest understanding of the real 80/20 rule would have scoffed at the leadership mania early on, knowing that 80% of the population is mediocre. Just because everyone born in this country can become president doesn't mean that everyone is presidential material.

Still, the tired phrase, "It's a matter of leadership," lingers on. It was a favorite of conservatives in their critique of President Obama when they were not accusing him of being an overreaching tyrant. (Isn't it amazing how quickly they changed their tune regarding presidential overreach when Donald Trump took office.) Their followers bought the diatribes of FOX media heads lock, stock and barrel. I doubt that most of them had the slightest inkling of how meaningless their charges were.

On the other hand, it never occurs to them either how little those in charge really know. You may have heard of President George Bush Sr.'s amazement at the existence of scanners in a supermarket? It was a precious moment. He'd never seen one before—that is, the inside of a grocery store.

The way to mess with others for their own good is to turn these hackneyed phrases on their head. Tell them that in times of trouble, "It's a matter of good followership."

Or let people know that you're writing a book called, "Developing the Follower Inside You."

Or remind them, as one of my friends likes to say, "If your leader's a schmo, he's a schmo."

RELATIONSHIPS

Everyone knows that women are different from men, and vice versa, and that they will never understand one another completely (I'm talking cisgender here). This state of affairs requires patience, tolerance and a good sense of humor, on both sides, to make the world go round and develop good relationships.

Take something as simple as women's ability to wrap their heads in a towel after a shower, turban-like, and have it hold together without safety pins and glue. They all know how to do this, as if it were part of their genetic make-up.

Most men would not be caught dead doing that, even if they were capable of performing such a feat, and they'd probably need duct tape to pull it off. They barely know how to wrap the towel around their waist and cinch it tight with a simple corner tuck. By then, they have used the towel to rub their hair dry enough for a comb, brush or electric dryer and are ready to scratch whatever part of their anatomy needs special attention.

Here's another topic to boggle the mind: Why does it still matter to so many women whether or not men put the toilet seat down after peeing (this can lead to heated discussions in workplaces with unisex bathrooms)? They keep trying to make it an issue of male insensitivity. But really, what's the big deal? In these post-feminist times, you'd think we'd come to a point of parity on this one—whoever uses the toilet adjust it to his or her needs and leaves it at that. You don't hear guys complaining about having to raise the seat to do their business.

Cisgender men and women also occupy different realms of space. I know it's politically incorrect to claim that women are more direction-challenged than men. Guys are the ones who won't ask for directions when they're lost, but they don't go off course as often. There's even research suggesting that male and female brains are wired differently to back up the contention that men, as a group, are better at spacial relationships. In any case, no one can deny the positive impact of the invention of the GPS on both genders. It helps women reach their destinations easily; and for men, who are masters at tuning out women talking, it's probably the only time they'll actually listen to and follow the advice of a female voice. Well, that and Siri and Alexa.

SEX

I have only three things to say on the subject:

1. Good sex, like good food, good wine and good company is divine.

2. Size, contrary to general opinion, does not matter (it does in many other walks of life, but that's another story.)

3. Slow is better than fast, especially as you get older and more mature.

Mention any of these in polite conversation, and you'll be messing with people's heads in a very good way. Some of them will giggle, uncontrollably. Since, thanks to our Puritan forbears, we're a society obsessed with sex and confused about it at the same time, reminding people how good and pleasurable it can be is quite liberating.

MULTITASKING

In the vein of "You can have all, baby!" the laurels heaped on multitasking is one of the more inane practices inflicted on the general populace. People are supposed to beam with pride at their abilities to walk, chew gum, and text at the same time. But I'm with my friend Kate Brown on this one. She's a professional organizer, and her comment on the subject is, "Multitasking makes you stupid!" (Not as in "Dare to be stupid," but as in "Don't be bibulous, addlepate stupid.")

That is not to say that you can't *do* more than one thing at a time. Our bodies are capable of juggling a number of tasks simultaneously. So long as our conscious awareness doesn't get involved. If we had to multi-task breathing, digestion and blood circulation with full attentiveness, cockroaches would have taken over the world long ago, because we wouldn't be around.

Let's face it, we are a one-thing-after-another creature, incapable of holding onto more than one thought or perception at a time. When you think of one thing, you can't think of another. Ask yourself after you've been blithely yakking away on your cell phone while operating a motor vehicle, how much you remember of the drive. Be honest. The answer is: None of it! Because you were on autopilot during the call.

That doesn't mean you can't work on more than one project at a time. Isaac Asimov, the famous sci-fi writer who penned nearly 400 books in his lifetime, had several typewriters in his office—this was before computers came along—and he would go from one book he was working on to the next as the spirit moved him.

How To Mess With Others For Their Own Good

The key is to learn how to focus intently on one thing at a time, not an easy task in an ADD challenged world. Once you've mastered that, feel free to flit around like a butterfly from one flower to the next.

Knowing this will help you mess with others. Since most people are as easily distracted as children, you can redirect their attention. All you have to do in a crowd is point to the sky and say, "Oh my God, look up! There!" and watch people's heads tilt back, regardless of what they're doing!

So if someone is in a maudlin mood, overzealously arguing, or boring others with a detailed description of their favorite hobby—read: beating a dead horse to a pulp—just divert their attention, and you'll have done them (and their captive audience) a world of good!

WORRY, WORRY, WORRY

The world must be one dull and ordinary place for many. Why else would people spend so much time watching and reading about the peccadilloes and problems of Hollywood movie stars, super athletes and randy politicians? Or pour out their hearts over the death of Princess Di or Michael Jackson or the current tragedy du jour?

I'm always amused when someone like Paris Hilton or Lindsay Lohan or Snowplow Mom Felicity Huffman is sent to jail or rehab, and the media descend like piranhas in a feeding frenzy. You can be sure that in no time there will be talking heads bemoaning the fact that so much airtime is being spent on a nonentity with an enhanced body, bleached skin, or a trust fund. But they'll run the latest footage of the celebs in trouble behind the news report over and over and over, all the while complaining about how our society is going to the dogs.

They never ask the interesting questions. If so many people are fascinated by royalty, if they want to hear about the latest sheenanigans of Kim Kardashian and other no talents who are famous only by accident of birth and a shameless drive for celebrity, what purpose does the fascination serve in their lives? What's in it for them? That will get us closer to a real conversation about the nature of deprivation, desperation and depression in our society.

Which brings me to worrying. There are people who make themselves sick with worry. They fuss and wriggle and worry all the time, mostly over things they can do nothing about—the recent airplane crash on another continent, the weather, their favorite sports team in a slump. It's not just an American thing. In the late 1950s and 60s, people world-wide worried about the A-bomb and the Ruskies—but what effect did that have on the situation?

I always tell these anxious fretters to start a worry journal. The idea is not original with me, but suggesting it others to mess with them for their own good, probably is.

Let me be clear here: I'm not suggesting *you* keep a worry journal. I'm encouraging you to tell *others* to do so.

In the old days, there were scapegoats and whipping boys. The former took on all the sins and evils of a village or society and got sacrificed. The latter stood in for the children of royalty who couldn't be touched or physically punished by a lesser mortal when they screwed up. If the prince committed a boo-boo, it was the whipping boy that got his hide tanned.

However primitive and medieval these practices were, they served a useful purpose. Sins and misbehavior are burdensome, especially if you have to carry them with you. Better to find a way to rid yourself of them. Same thing with worries. It takes a lot of energy to tote them around in your head and heart.

Since we don't have a designated worry wart to do all our agonizing for us, I suggest that keeping a notebook, a pad or a roll of paper handy will do just as well. Here's the recipe: Whenever they find themselves worrying about something or other—big and little things—they should write it down right away. As soon as possible after it enters their mind.

Have them do this for a month.

It will be a life-changing experience because they'll discover that more than 95% of their worries don't come true. Some of them will even realize that excessive fretting is an ineffective and wasteful way to occupy their time and energy and stop worrying altogether.

When I suggest to people to do this, they invariably say, "That's an interesting idea. I should try that." And of course, they never do. But it gives me the opportunity to mess with them some more the next time I see them: "How are you coming with your worry journal?"

Plus, once I have given them the suggestions, they stop burdening me with their concerns. After all, why should I worry about their worries with them?

And neither should you!

There is one issue facing us globally that *is* alarming: Climate change. But even with a threat so existential to our planet and our way of life, unless you're prepared to wade in and try to do something about it —I'm speaking about big picture change, not individualistic attempts to minimize your carbon footprint—best to not to worry about it all the time. Not everyone can be a Greta Thunberg, the Swedish climate activist, whose campaign on the issue since she was 15 has made considerable international impact.

When people get strident about the end of the world, one way to take the wind out of their sails is to take an Olympian perspective, as the son of a friend of mine frequently does. When people try to bend his ear with their apocalyptical anxieties, he shrugs sympathetically and says, "It's only life as we know it."

It usually takes people a moment or two to get it.

THREE QUESTIONS

A good friend who likes to mess with people as much as I do often poses one or more of these questions at parties and get-togethers. Sometimes he's met with puzzlement, awkward silence and befuddled stares. But at other times, it stops people in their conversational ruts and opens up new avenues of stimulating discussions.

Is the universe fundamentally a positive or negative place?

Many will try to hedge here and say, "That depends," or "Well, sometimes it's one, sometimes the other," or they bail and insist, "Both." Push them up against the wall and require them to make a choice. Which way they go will reveal multitudes about them.

If there is a heaven, what would you want it to look like when you die?

Encourage visuals—and let people know that harps and clouds don't count. Nor does having your way with 40 virgins.

If God made us in his image, does the creator have both male and female sex organs?

This one takes some courage to hoist on the flag pole to see if anyone will salute. I recommend posing this question only after people have become comfortable with you or have had several beers or glasses of wine.

WHITE AND BLACK HATS

America is a very Cartesian society. We like simple dualities—mind/body, up/down, innocence and guilt, good and evil, Republicans and Democrats (despite many people's understandable disgust with both parties). When Westerns were still a popular movie genre, good guys wore white hats and villains wore black.

Any gray areas make people nervous.

So it is perfectly normal to divide the world into dogs and cats. Since they are the most popular pets, and owners often take after their animals, we can also divide the world into people who're either dogs or cats.

Dogs are a little easier to understand and get along with. Just think about phrases we use in relation to others, as in "You dog, you!" Or, "He's a real hound." Or, "He showed dogged determination." In part that's because dogs are simpler creatures. They run in packs. They want to be social, horse around with you, be your best friend.

Understanding felines is more difficult because cats are more complicated. They can be stand-offish and harder to read. And they've gotten a bad rep. There is "You pussy!" Hardly a compliment. And "pussy-footing, around," "Cat's got your tongue?" and "Curiosity killed the cat."

Still, once we recognize the differences between the two species, we'll quickly understand what kind of people we're talking about: happy-go-lucky, galumphing party animals vs. prickly loners with an attitude. (I'm simplifying, of course, but remember stereotypes—they work for groups even if they don't apply to every individual.)

People who lead with their emotions—dogs.

People who favor their intellect—cats.

People who like rock 'n roll and country music—dogs.
People that go for classical music or jazz—cats—hep cats, if you will.
And so on.

Knowing this will allow you to relate to them accordingly. Approach a dog with effusive expressions of love, and he will happily bounce up and down with you. Do the same to a cat, and she's likely to hiss, scram in the other direction and find a special hiding place; and refuse to make another appearance until you're gone. With cats you have to take a subtler, more indirect approach.

Cats and dogs—they make the world go round.

Once you've established this obvious duality, you can start to mess with people for their own good by saying things like:

On the third hand, there are birds…you dodo!

And reptiles…you snake!

And insects….

Remember, the more truths you have, the better.

CONCLUSION

The methods described in this book can be used for good or ill. Most of the nightmares of history have been caused by clever and ruthless people who knew how to mess with others in order to manipulate them or to consolidate power. All the great destructive isms of the 19th and 20th centuries—socialism, Communism, Fascism—which asserted that they would create a better human being, were hijacked by demagogues, expert at messing with others. And who knew a thing or two about repression, too.

Capitalism, while it makes no such lofty claims, suffers from the same fundamental problem as the others—great in theory; but in practice, not so much. Flesh and blood humans always gum up the works, often to the detriment of others, as the self-serving executives of Lehman Brothers, Goldman Sachs and other invesment firms, and large banks amply demonstrated in the financial debacle that led to the Great Recession. There is something fundamentally wrong when it's possible to rake in lots of money by betting against a company or business succeeding, no matter how elegant the verbal acrobatics, algorhythms and contortions of capitalist spinmeisters and apologists.

Most of our current leaders lie, obfuscate and pursue interest in direct contradiction to what's good for the vast majority of the people they lead. That is as true in the United States as it is in other countries. And it goes for religion as much as politics. Nor is this a recent phenomenon. The will to power is as old as history. I'm with Lord Acton on this one: Power corrupts, and absolute power corrupts absolutely.

This book won't change that. But if you want to stay on the good side of ethics and live a decent life:

1. **It helps to like the people you're messing with. Your creativity will flow into kinder, more positive channels.**
2. **The idea is to mess with them, not to mess them over.**
3. **If you mess with others to their detriment, shame on you.**

So what does it all add up to? Besides fulminations about the idiocies committed by our leaders, power mongers and media stars. Of course, there isn't much else to do when the forces of inanity, shamelessness, greed, selfishness and incessant self-expression have the upper hand, as they currently do. To quote Karl Marx, "In times of counter-revolution, go to the library and heap abuse on your enemies."

It's also easy to mess with others, but only for *your* own good—a fine American tradition summed up by P.T. Barnum's comment, "There's a sucker born every minute."

But messing with others *for their own good* is a lot more difficult. Initially, it will take some thought. In time, it will get easier and you'll respond naturally as opportunities present themselves.

Here's a helpful hint. During the 1960s and 70s, the Esalen Institute in Big Sur, California, an alternative humanistic education organization, used to teach that any communication from another person is either a message of love or a cry for help.

Looking at the world this way, can open up surprising paths of understanding and, perhaps, teach you to let your messing with others for their own good be a positive message.

If that doesn't work for you, I recommend starting by giving lots of verbal advice to others.

Just don't expect them to take it, and you'll be all right.

ACKNOWLEDGMENTS

There are many whose wisdom and irreverence has influenced me, but I want to give special thanks to the following:

Dr. Michael Dorociak, a dentist with a rare sense of humor. Trying out for the TV show *Survivor*, he submitted a video in which he backed a cement truck and shute up to the mouth of one of his patients for a concrete filling.

James Wimsatt, who told me when I was in my 20s and the throes of *Weltschmerz*, a German affliction of the soul, rife with anguish, melancholy, and world-weariness, "You know, Chris, you're a very funny guy!" He introduced me to commedia del'arte and *The Goon Show* and taught me to appreciate the likes of George Carlin, George Burns, and Henny Youngman, the King of One-Liners, and all the other wonderful comedians who use humor to mess with others for their own good.

Ed Linehan, whose friendship and wicked Irish humor has inspired me for more than 50 years.

My wife **Susan**, who is the wisest reader and critic of my work and puts up with my running commentary and yelling at the television when I get upset at the willful ignorance, hypocrisy, vulgarity, racism, prejudice and intolerance of so many of our political leaders. She reminds me, gently, to heed my own advice and take more measured approach.

For more information and additional ways
to mess with others for their own good, go to:

www.chrisangermann.com

www.ingramcontent.com/pod-product-compliance
Lightning Source LLC
Chambersburg PA
CBHW071238090426
42736CB00014B/3134